#NeverTicket
How to never EVER get a speeding ticket

Jonathan C. Elrod

Jonathan Elrod

DEDICATION

This book is dedicated to all of the parents of teenage drivers who diligently teach their kids how to drive, and stay up sleepless nights worrying that one day they will get the call that they have been dreading. The call that comes after curfew has passed. The call that will change things for their household. The call that your teenage driver makes to tell you he has received his first speeding ticket, and your insurance rates will *never* be the same! It doesn't have to happen!

Jonathan Elrod

INTRODUCTION

I was moved to write this book because I am a parent, and my oldest child has recently obtained his learners permit. This is a big deal! Being that my teen is no different from other teenagers in a lack of judgment and proper application of common sense, I felt the need to really spell things out on how driving works, especially relating to speeding and tickets, so that nothing was left to his own interpretation. I researched tirelessly my own states driving laws so that I could pass on the right advice. Then I realized that my son had friends that were getting their learners permits as well and I wanted to make sure they could all benefit from the same common sense advice. Then I realized teens all over the country needed this advice! So I reviewed the laws in all 50 states so that everyone in the country, not just the continental US, could take advantage of it.

This book has a chapter dedicated for each state, and is organized in alphabetical order for your convenience. And don't worry, the information is written in a way that your teen won't possibly miss the important stuff, and you may even benefit from this as well as you strive to never get a speeding ticket again!

Your teen driver won't have to worry about construction zones, small town speed traps or even those automatic speeding ticket cameras that are intrusively showing up everywhere. If your state specific advice is followed, you will all enjoy a **#NeverTicket** life!

Jonathan Elrod

CONTENTS

23	Minnesota	23
24	Mississippi	24
25	Missouri	25
26	Montana	26
27	Nebraska	27
28	Nevada	28
29	New Hampshire	29
30	New Jersey	30
31	New Mexico	31
32	New York	32
33	North Carolina	33
34	North Dakota	34
35	Ohio	35
36	Oklahoma	36
37	Oregon	37
38	Pennsylvania	38
39	Rhode Island	39
40	South Carolina	40
41	South Dakota	41
42	Tennessee	42
43	Texas	43
44	Utah	44
45	Vermont	45
46	Virginia	46
47	Washington	47

DISCLAIMER

ALABAMA

Sweet home Alabama! To never get a speeding ticket while driving in Alabama, it is quite simple:

ALWAYS OBEY POSTED SPEED LIMITS!!!

Follow this simple rule and you will enjoy a #NeverTicket life! Insurance rates will not increase, chance of vehicle damage are greatly reduced, and your life expectancy will go up! Life will be good.

ALASKA

Home of the ice road truckers! To never get a speeding ticket while driving in Alaska, it is quite simple regardless of your skill on the ice:

ALWAYS OBEY POSTED SPEED LIMITS!!!

Follow this simple rule and you will enjoy a #NeverTicket life! Insurance rates will not increase, chance of vehicle damage are greatly reduced, and your life expectancy will go up! Life will be good.

ARIZONA

To never get a speeding ticket while driving to visit the Grand Canyon in Arizona, it is quite simple:

ALWAYS OBEY POSTED SPEED LIMITS!!!

Follow this simple rule and you will enjoy a #NeverTicket life! Insurance rates will not increase, chance of vehicle damage are greatly reduced, and your life expectancy will go up! Life will be good.

ARKANSAS

Home of Sam Walton and his retail juggernaut! To never get a speeding ticket while driving in Arkansas, it is quite simple:

ALWAYS OBEY POSTED SPEED LIMITS!!!

Follow this simple rule and you will enjoy a #NeverTicket life! Insurance rates will not increase, chance of vehicle damage are greatly reduced, and your life expectancy will go up! Life will be good.

CALIFORNIA

When driving the scenic coasts of California you have to remember two things. First, brace yourselves for earthquakes. Secondly and most importantly:

ALWAYS OBEY POSTED SPEED LIMITS!!!

Follow this simple rule and you will enjoy a #NeverTicket life! Insurance rates will not increase, chance of vehicle damage are greatly reduced, and your life expectancy will go up! Life will be good.

COLORADO

If you find yourself in the Mile High state, and you better not be high regardless of the marijuana laws, the best way to never get a speeding ticket is to:

ALWAYS OBEY POSTED SPEED LIMITS!!!

Follow this simple rule and you will enjoy a #NeverTicket life! Insurance rates will not increase, chance of vehicle damage are greatly reduced, and your life expectancy will go up! Life will be good.

CONNECTICUT

The law professors of Yale couldn't give you more solid advice than this in order to never get a speeding ticket:

ALWAYS OBEY POSTED SPEED LIMITS!!!

Follow this simple rule and you will enjoy a #NeverTicket life! Insurance rates will not increase, chance of vehicle damage are greatly reduced, and your life expectancy will go up! Life will be good.

DELEWARE

If you are driving in the First State, there is only one thing to remember in order to never get a speeding ticket:

ALWAYS OBEY POSTED SPEED LIMITS!!!

Follow this simple rule and you will enjoy a #NeverTicket life! Insurance rates will not increase, chance of vehicle damage are greatly reduced, and your life expectancy will go up! Life will be good.

FLORIDA

If you are driving in the Sunshine state and are looking for fun in the sun on endless beaches and amusement parks, there is only one thing to remember in order to never get a speeding ticket:

ALWAYS OBEY POSTED SPEED LIMITS!!!

Follow this simple rule and you will enjoy a #NeverTicket life! Insurance rates will not increase, chance of vehicle damage are greatly reduced, and your life expectancy will go up! Life will be good.

GEORGIA

If you've got Georgia on your mind, southern hospitality won't get you out of a speeding ticket. In Georgia there is only one thing to remember in order to never get a speeding ticket:

ALWAYS OBEY POSTED SPEED LIMITS!!!

Follow this simple rule and you will enjoy a #NeverTicket life! Insurance rates will not increase, chance of vehicle damage are greatly reduced, and your life expectancy will go up! Life will be good.

HAWAII

Aloha! If you think you're the Big Kahuna in town and think you can weasel your way out to a speeding ticket, think again. In Hawaii there is only one thing to do in order to never get a speeding ticket:

ALWAYS OBEY POSTED SPEED LIMITS!!!

Follow this simple rule and you will enjoy a #NeverTicket life! Insurance rates will not increase, chance of vehicle damage are greatly reduced, and your life expectancy will go up! Life will be good.

IDAHO

If find yourself driving in Idaho I will give you a bonus tip that has nothing to do with traffic law, and I will do it without the obligatory mention of potatoes. Don't give anyone a gift of a box of candy that weights more than 50 pounds. That is illegal there. And in Idaho there is only one thing to remember in order to never get a speeding ticket:

ALWAYS OBEY POSTED SPEED LIMITS!!!

Follow this simple rule and you will enjoy a #NeverTicket life! Insurance rates will not increase, chance of vehicle damage are greatly reduced, and your life expectancy will go up! Life will be good.

ILLINOIS

If you're in Illinois you have the greatest pizza on Earth, and mobsters to boot! You will need to pay special consideration to this advice to avoid a speeding ticket here. In Illinois there is only one thing to remember in order to never get a speeding ticket from the likes of Eliot Ness:

ALWAYS OBEY POSTED SPEED LIMITS!!!

Follow this simple rule and you will enjoy a #NeverTicket life! Insurance rates will not increase, chance of vehicle damage are greatly reduced, and your life expectancy will go up! Life will be good.

INDIANA

In Indiana, you love your basketball. But even if you are the team captain of the Hoosiers there is only one thing to remember in order to never get a speeding ticket:

ALWAYS OBEY POSTED SPEED LIMITS!!!

Follow this simple rule and you will enjoy a #NeverTicket life! Insurance rates will not increase, chance of vehicle damage are greatly reduced, and your life expectancy will go up! Life will be good.

IOWA

In Iowa, once every 4 years the eyes of the nation are on you as you kick off the national political campaigns. If you are a candidate on the trail, or a delicate on the way to a caucus there is only one thing to remember in order to never get a speeding ticket:

ALWAYS OBEY POSTED SPEED LIMITS!!!

Follow this simple rule and you will enjoy a #NeverTicket life! Insurance rates will not increase, chance of vehicle damage are greatly reduced, and your life expectancy will go up! Life will be good.

KANSAS

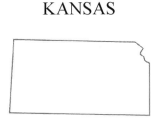

In Kansas, be careful of tornadoes and wicked witches, don't look to Todo for advice. The most important to remember in order to never get a speeding ticket:

ALWAYS OBEY POSTED SPEED LIMITS!!!

Follow this simple rule and you will enjoy a #NeverTicket life! Insurance rates will not increase, chance of vehicle damage are greatly reduced, and your life expectancy will go up! Life will be good.

KENTUCKY

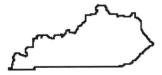

In Kentucky, the roads are no derby! The most important to remember right out of the gate in order to never get a speeding ticket:

ALWAYS OBEY POSTED SPEED LIMITS!!!

Follow this simple rule and you will enjoy a #NeverTicket life! Insurance rates will not increase, chance of vehicle damage are greatly reduced, and your life expectancy will go up! Life will be good.

LOUISIANA

In Louisiana, the swamps offer a multitude of adventurous activities. The most important to remember on the bayou in order to never get a speeding ticket:

ALWAYS OBEY POSTED SPEED LIMITS!!!

Follow this simple rule and you will enjoy a #NeverTicket life! Insurance rates will not increase, chance of vehicle damage are greatly reduced, and your life expectancy will go up! Life will be good.

MAINE

In Maine, I am told that there are no poisonous snakes. The most important thing to remember in our northern most contiguous state in order to never get a speeding ticket:

ALWAYS OBEY POSTED SPEED LIMITS!!!

Follow this simple rule and you will enjoy a #NeverTicket life! Insurance rates will not increase, chance of vehicle damage are greatly reduced, and your life expectancy will go up! Life will be good.

MARYLAND

You may enjoy sailing in Chesapeake Bay, but on land the most important thing to remember in order to never get a speeding ticket:

ALWAYS OBEY POSTED SPEED LIMITS!!!

Follow this simple rule and you will enjoy a #NeverTicket life! Insurance rates will not increase, chance of vehicle damage are greatly reduced, and your life expectancy will go up! Life will be good.

MASSACHUSETTS

Massachusetts is rich in American history. When the pilgrims landed on Plymouth, they knew that the most important thing to remember in order to never get a speeding ticket:

ALWAYS OBEY POSTED SPEED LIMITS!!!

Follow this simple rule and you will enjoy a #NeverTicket life! Insurance rates will not increase, chance of vehicle damage are greatly reduced, and your life expectancy will go up! Life will be good.

MICHIGAN

You may be tempted to go fast when you drive through Motor City, but the most important thing to remember in order to never get a speeding ticket:

ALWAYS OBEY POSTED SPEED LIMITS!!!

Follow this simple rule and you will enjoy a #NeverTicket life! Insurance rates will not increase, chance of vehicle damage are greatly reduced, and your life expectancy will go up! Life will be good.

MINNESOTA

Minnesota is the beautiful land of a thousand lakes, but only one rule will keep you from getting a speeding ticket:

ALWAYS OBEY POSTED SPEED LIMITS!!!

Follow this simple rule and you will enjoy a #NeverTicket life! Insurance rates will not increase, chance of vehicle damage are greatly reduced, and your life expectancy will go up! Life will be good.

MISSISSIPPI

ISSISSIPPIM

I can spell this as fast backwards as I can forwards, but that won't be able to dazzle the police. There is only one rule will keep you from getting a speeding ticket:

ALWAYS OBEY POSTED SPEED LIMITS!!!

Follow this simple rule and you will enjoy a #NeverTicket life! Insurance rates will not increase, chance of vehicle damage are greatly reduced, and your life expectancy will go up! Life will be good.

MISSOURI

If you are in the "Show Me" state and don't want an officer to say, "Show me your license and registration", this one rule will keep that from happening:

ALWAYS OBEY POSTED SPEED LIMITS!!!

Follow this simple rule and you will enjoy a #NeverTicket life! Insurance rates will not increase, chance of vehicle damage are greatly reduced, and your life expectancy will go up! Life will be good.

NEBRASKA

For driving in Nebraska its simple. This one rule will keep you from getting a speeding ticket:

ALWAYS OBEY POSTED SPEED LIMITS!!!

Follow this simple rule and you will enjoy a #NeverTicket life! Insurance rates will not increase, chance of vehicle damage are greatly reduced, and your life expectancy will go up! Life will be good.

NEVADA

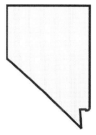

Think you're a high roller driving through the strip? Think again. This one rule will keep you from getting a speeding ticket:

ALWAYS OBEY POSTED SPEED LIMITS!!!

Follow this simple rule and you will enjoy a #NeverTicket life! Insurance rates will not increase, chance of vehicle damage are greatly reduced, and your life expectancy will go up! Life will be good.

NEW HAMPSHIRE

Live free or die. But not so free that you don't follow this one rule will keep you from getting a speeding ticket:

ALWAYS OBEY POSTED SPEED LIMITS!!!

Follow this simple rule and you will enjoy a #NeverTicket life! Insurance rates will not increase, chance of vehicle damage are greatly reduced, and your life expectancy will go up! Life will be good.

NEW JERSEY

When you are causing on the Jersey shore, following this one rule will keep you from getting a speeding ticket:

ALWAYS OBEY POSTED SPEED LIMITS!!!

Follow this simple rule and you will enjoy a #NeverTicket life! Insurance rates will not increase, chance of vehicle damage are greatly reduced, and your life expectancy will go up! Life will be good.

NEW MEXICO

If you are a driver in New Mexico, following this one rule will keep you from getting a speeding ticket:

ALWAYS OBEY POSTED SPEED LIMITS!!!

Follow this simple rule and you will enjoy a #NeverTicket life! Insurance rates will not increase, chance of vehicle damage are greatly reduced, and your life expectancy will go up! Life will be good.

NEW YORK

The Big Apple is a unique place, and following this one rule will keep you from getting a speeding ticket:

ALWAYS OBEY POSTED SPEED LIMITS!!!

Follow this simple rule and you will enjoy a #NeverTicket life! Insurance rates will not increase, chance of vehicle damage are greatly reduced, and your life expectancy will go up! Life will be good.

NORTH CAROLINA

If you are in North Carolina and enjoying the scenic Blue Ridge Parkway, following this one rule will keep you from getting a speeding ticket:

ALWAYS OBEY POSTED SPEED LIMITS!!!

Follow this simple rule and you will enjoy a #NeverTicket life! Insurance rates will not increase, chance of vehicle damage are greatly reduced, and your life expectancy will go up! Life will be good.

NORTH DAKOTA

If you are in North Dakota, you are the first line of defense if the Canadians decide to invade. In the mean time, to keep from getting a speeding ticket follow this one rule:

ALWAYS OBEY POSTED SPEED LIMITS!!!

Follow this simple rule and you will enjoy a #NeverTicket life! Insurance rates will not increase, chance of vehicle damage are greatly reduced, and your life expectancy will go up! Life will be good.

OHIO

The laws in Ohio are amazingly simple. To keep from getting a speeding ticket follow this one rule:

ALWAYS OBEY POSTED SPEED LIMITS!!!

Follow this simple rule and you will enjoy a #NeverTicket life! Insurance rates will not increase, chance of vehicle damage are greatly reduced, and your life expectancy will go up! Life will be good.

OKLAHOMA

If you are a driver in Oklahoma, your states laws are really quite clear. To keep from getting a speeding ticket follow this one rule:

ALWAYS OBEY POSTED SPEED LIMITS!!!

Follow this simple rule and you will enjoy a #NeverTicket life! Insurance rates will not increase, chance of vehicle damage are greatly reduced, and your life expectancy will go up! Life will be good.

OREGON

If you are a Millennial, ask your parents about their experience on the Oregon trail. Since that time the laws have changed. To keep from getting a speeding ticket follow this one rule:

ALWAYS OBEY POSTED SPEED LIMITS!!!

Follow this simple rule and you will enjoy a #NeverTicket life! Insurance rates will not increase, chance of vehicle damage are greatly reduced, and your life expectancy will go up! Life will be good.

PENNSYLVANIA

If you are driving in the Quaker, you need to watch out for horse and buggies, and if you don't want a speeding ticket follow this one rule:

ALWAYS OBEY POSTED SPEED LIMITS!!!

Follow this simple rule and you will enjoy a #NeverTicket life! Insurance rates will not increase, chance of vehicle damage are greatly reduced, and your life expectancy will go up! Life will be good.

RHODE ISLAND

Being that Rhode Island is the smallest state in the union, if you find your-self speeding you will probably pass right through it! However if you don't want a speeding ticket follow this one rule:

ALWAYS OBEY POSTED SPEED LIMITS!!!

Follow this simple rule and you will enjoy a #NeverTicket life! Insurance rates will not increase, chance of vehicle damage are greatly reduced, and your life expectancy will go up! Life will be good.

SOUTH CAROLINA

South Carolina drivers are no different than North Carolina Drivers. If you don't want a speeding ticket follow this one rule:

ALWAYS OBEY POSTED SPEED LIMITS!!!

Follow this simple rule and you will enjoy a #NeverTicket life! Insurance rates will not increase, chance of vehicle damage are greatly reduced, and your life expectancy will go up! Life will be good.

SOUTH DAKOTA

If you are in South Dakota, the presidents are watching you from the mountain. To keep from getting a speeding ticket follow this one rule:

ALWAYS OBEY POSTED SPEED LIMITS!!!

Follow this simple rule and you will enjoy a #NeverTicket life! Insurance rates will not increase, chance of vehicle damage are greatly reduced, and your life expectancy will go up! Life will be good.

TENNESSEE

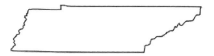

If you are learning to drive in "Music City", to keep from getting a speeding ticket follow this one rule:

ALWAYS OBEY POSTED SPEED LIMITS!!!

Follow this simple rule and you will enjoy a #NeverTicket life! Insurance rates will not increase, chance of vehicle damage are greatly reduced, and your life expectancy will go up! Life will be good.

TEXAS

The Lone Star state the eyes of the Ranger are upon you, so to keep from getting a speeding ticket follow this one rule:

ALWAYS OBEY POSTED SPEED LIMITS!!!

Follow this simple rule and you will enjoy a #NeverTicket life! Insurance rates will not increase, chance of vehicle damage are greatly reduced, and your life expectancy will go up! Life will be good.

UTAH

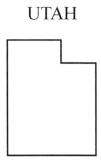

Unless you are trying to set a new world land speed record on the salt flats, to keep from getting a speeding ticket follow this one rule:

ALWAYS OBEY POSTED SPEED LIMITS!!!

Follow this simple rule and you will enjoy a #NeverTicket life! Insurance rates will not increase, chance of vehicle damage are greatly reduced, and your life expectancy will go up! Life will be good.

VERMONT

When driving in Vermont, the law is actually quite simple. To keep from getting a speeding ticket follow this one rule:

ALWAYS OBEY POSTED SPEED LIMITS!!!

Follow this simple rule and you will enjoy a #NeverTicket life! Insurance rates will not increase, chance of vehicle damage are greatly reduced, and your life expectancy will go up! Life will be good.

VIRGINIA

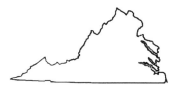

When driving in the birthplace of the nation, keep in mind how easy it is to never get a speeding ticket:

ALWAYS OBEY POSTED SPEED LIMITS!!!

Follow this simple rule and you will enjoy a #NeverTicket life! Insurance rates will not increase, chance of vehicle damage are greatly reduced, and your life expectancy will go up! Life will be good.

WASHINGTON

When driving in Washington state, you get more than your share of rainy road conditions. To never get a speeding ticket:

ALWAYS OBEY POSTED SPEED LIMITS!!!

Follow this simple rule and you will enjoy a #NeverTicket life! Insurance rates will not increase, chance of vehicle damage are greatly reduced, and your life expectancy will go up! Life will be good.

WEST VIRGINIA

You may not just be a coal miners daughter, but to never get a speeding ticket:

ALWAYS OBEY POSTED SPEED LIMITS!!!

Follow this simple rule and you will enjoy a #NeverTicket life! Insurance rates will not increase, chance of vehicle damage are greatly reduced, and your life expectancy will go up! Life will be good.

WISCONSIN

Cheese-heads have to pay special attention to driving with your big cheese hats. So to never get a speeding ticket:

ALWAYS OBEY POSTED SPEED LIMITS!!!

Follow this simple rule and you will enjoy a #NeverTicket life! Insurance rates will not increase, chance of vehicle damage are greatly reduced, and your life expectancy will go up! Life will be good.

WYOMING

The beauty of Wyoming can be very distracting, so you will have to pay extra attention. To never get a speeding ticket:

ALWAYS OBEY POSTED SPEED LIMITS!!!

Follow this simple rule and you will enjoy a #NeverTicket life! Insurance rates will not increase, chance of vehicle damage are greatly reduced, and your life expectancy will go up! Life will be good.

BONUS CHAPTER
WASHINGTON D.C.

Not actually a state, our nations capitol has some horrendous driving conditions. To never get a speeding ticket:

ALWAYS OBEY POSTED SPEED LIMITS!!!

Follow this simple rule and you will enjoy a #NeverTicket life! Insurance rates will not increase, chance of vehicle damage are greatly reduced, and your life expectancy will go up! Life will be good.

Bonus Tip:

Bonus tip for drivers in Washington D.C. If you are an elected official headed to an official vote, you can't be stopped! So while you are observing all posted speed limits, be on the look out for crazy politicians driving dangerously.

CONCLUSION

The advice in this book is pretty obvious if you haven't figured that out already. But if you are still struggling, here are some figures that may help you live a **#NeverTicket** life.

Part of living a #NeverTicket life is passing along the message. So sign the log book below, and pass it along to a friend who needs to hear this message. No telling where this book will end up, and who will have signed it. And one day it may come back to you:

Name	State	Month/Year

Name	State	Month/Year

Name	State	Month/Year

Name	State	Month/Year

Name	State	Month/Year

Made in the USA
Middletown, DE
13 December 2022

18402192R00068